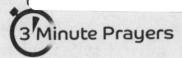

G000144764

3'Minute Prayers

3 Minute Prayers

FOR THE MORNING

GAYNOR COBB

kevin mayhew

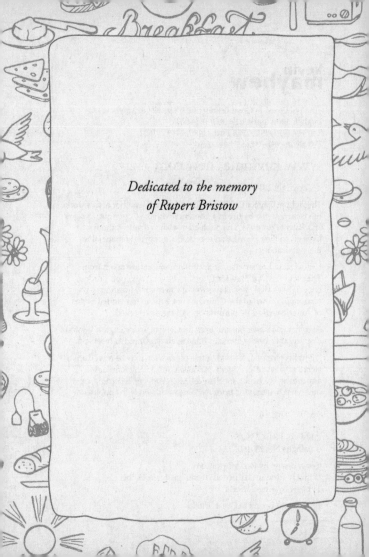

*Dedicated to the memory
of Rupert Bristow*

kevin
mayhew

First published in Great Britain in 2019 by Kevin Mayhew Ltd
Buxhall, Stowmarket, Suffolk IP14 3BW
Tel: +44 (0) 1449 737978 Fax: +44 (0) 1449 737834
E-mail: info@kevinmayhew.com

www.kevinmayhew.com

Unless stated otherwise, Scripture quotations are taken from
The New Revised Standard Version Bible: Anglicised Edition,
copyright © 1989, 1995, Division of Christian Education of the
National Council of the Churches of Christ in the United States
of America. Used by permission. All rights reserved.

Scripture quotations are also from the Contemporary English Version®
Copyright © 1995 American Bible Society. All rights reserved.

9 8 7 6 5 4 3 2 1 0

ISBN 978 1 84867 982 5
Catalogue No. 1501603

Cover design by Rob Mortonson
© Image used under licence from Shutterstock Inc.
Typeset by Angela Selfe

Printed and bound in Great Britain

CONTENTS

Looking out of the window

Jesus

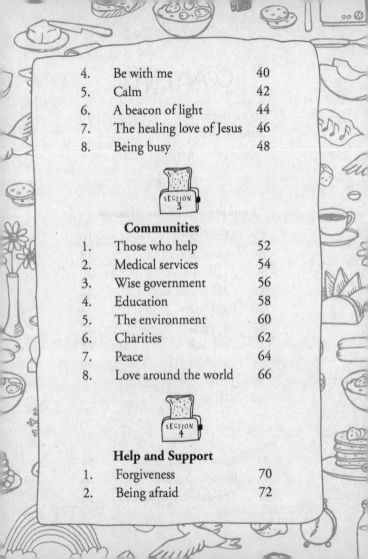

SECTION 3

Communities

SECTION 4

Help and Support

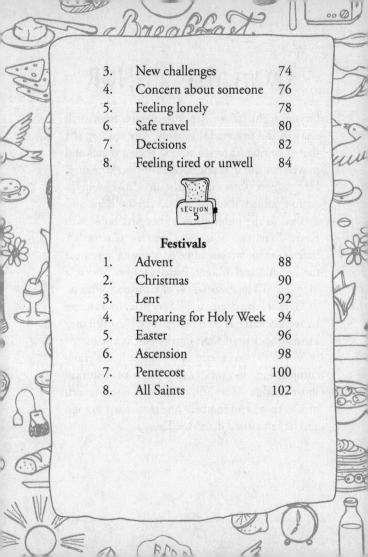

SECTION
5

Festivals

ABOUT THE AUTHOR

Gaynor Cobb has written intercessions for church services and prayers for schools. As a teacher, she started writing Christian stories, poetry, drama and prayers for use in schools, often for performance. Her project showing Christian Citizenship in Action gained the SACRE award in Kent and this led to the publication of her first book with Kevin Mayhew, *Teaching Christian Citizenship*. Later, Gaynor wrote online educational resources for Teachit and Career Paths Online. She is a member of The Association of Christian Writers.

Gaynor has a degree in History from Manchester University and has been secretary of New Romney History Society in Kent for the past ten years.

When she was awarded first prize in a writing competition, she produced a book of historical short stories. Her other interests include art, music, travel and football. She is married to John and has a married daughter, Laura.

INTRODUCTION

When we wake each morning, we prepare for the day ahead in many ways. Every day God gives us new opportunities to serve him and show his love to others.

If we are able to spend a few minutes in prayer, we will start the day refreshed, at peace with ourselves and ready to meet everything the day brings with calm and confidence, because we feel truly enfolded within God's love and guided by the loving friendship of our Saviour, Jesus Christ. In this way, we may be our best selves, reaching out to shine the light of Christ to all.

Here are prayers for special times of the year, for our world and local communities, and for mornings when we feel that we need help for ourselves or for others, along with prayers to match our mood when we look out of the window at the world outside. The prayers are supported by verses from the Bible, words of reflection and something extra to think about.

**Very early the next morning,
Jesus got up and went to a place
where he could be alone and pray.**

Mark 1:35 (CEV)

SECTION 1

LOOKING OUT OF
THE WINDOW

MORNING

**The steadfast love of the Lord never ceases,
his mercies never come to an end;
they are new every morning;
great is your faithfulness.**

Lamentations 3:22, 23

These verses are beautiful, although they come from one of the sad poems which lament the destruction of Jerusalem in 586 BC.

They remind us that God's love is not conditional, it is there every day, however we feel and whatever the circumstances. God never gives up on us. We can rely on him; even when things seem difficult, he will not desert us. As certain as the sun will rise every day, we can be sure of God's love; it is steadfast, real and exciting because God is love.

Just as we have a new day with a fresh morning, God's love for us is there and we can return that love by sharing it with others. We have new opportunities to celebrate God's love by following his word but whatever we do, he loves us and tomorrow will be another new day.

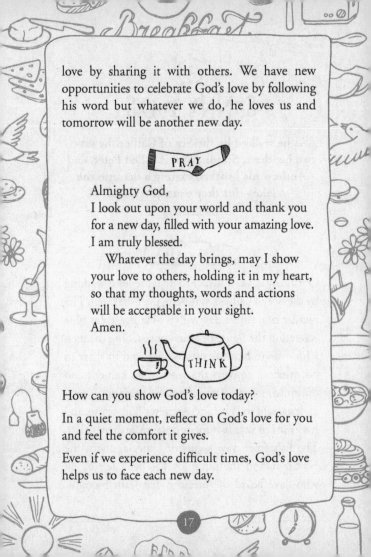

PRAY

Almighty God,
I look out upon your world and thank you for a new day, filled with your amazing love. I am truly blessed.
Whatever the day brings, may I show your love to others, holding it in my heart, so that my thoughts, words and actions will be acceptable in your sight.
Amen.

THINK

How can you show God's love today?

In a quiet moment, reflect on God's love for you and feel the comfort it gives.

Even if we experience difficult times, God's love helps us to face each new day.

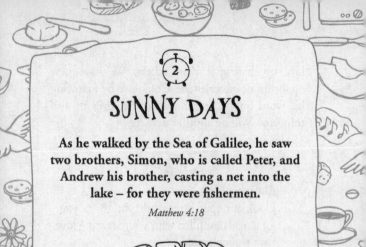

SUNNY DAYS

As he walked by the Sea of Galilee, he saw two brothers, Simon, who is called Peter, and Andrew his brother, casting a net into the lake – for they were fishermen.

Matthew 4:18

REFLECTION

On sunny days, it is easy to imagine Jesus walking by the Sea of Galilee, watching the fishermen. The picture of a sunlit day with a blue sky, calm blue water and the figure of Jesus approaching the men who were to become his disciples and to share in his mission, conveys the sense of excitement and optimism felt over two thousand years ago.

Jesus said to Peter and Andrew, 'Follow me, and I will make you fish for people' (Matthew 4:19). The fishermen saw something special about the Nazarene and the same joy has been felt by all who have heard the message that Jesus brought.

Jesus gives spiritual sunlight, shining God's love into our hearts every day.

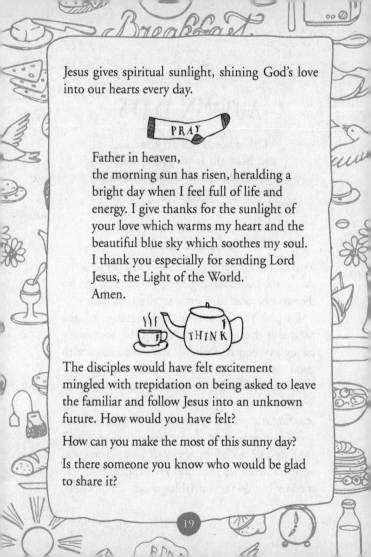

PRAY

Father in heaven,
the morning sun has risen, heralding a bright day when I feel full of life and energy. I give thanks for the sunlight of your love which warms my heart and the beautiful blue sky which soothes my soul. I thank you especially for sending Lord Jesus, the Light of the World.
Amen.

THINK

The disciples would have felt excitement mingled with trepidation on being asked to leave the familiar and follow Jesus into an unknown future. How would you have felt?

How can you make the most of this sunny day?

Is there someone you know who would be glad to share it?

AUTUMN DAYS

**Other seeds fell on good soil
and brought forth grain, some a
hundredfold, some sixty, some thirty.**

Matthew 13:8

REFLECTION

Jesus told The Parable of the Sower to a crowd at the side of the lake, speaking from a boat to people on the shore because so many wanted to hear him.

Despite the multitude, the message of the parable is that many people listen without really taking any notice of what is said. Some listen with good intentions but don't act on the message.

The seeds falling in good soil represent those who listen, understand and take heed of the message. The resulting corn varies, but there is a positive harvest.

How many times do we ask ourselves which seed we are? So often, we don't really listen and at other times we hear and even think about the message but don't do anything about it. Hopefully, there are times that we do take action because we read or listen to the word of God.

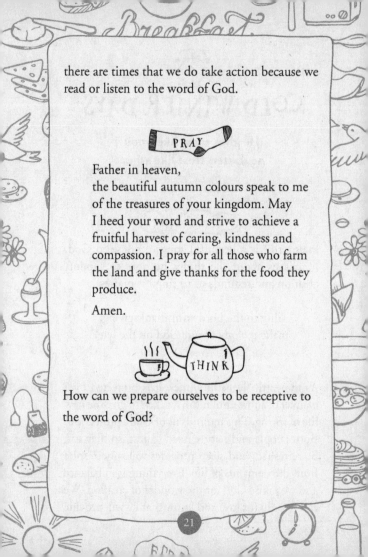

PRAY

Father in heaven,
the beautiful autumn colours speak to me
of the treasures of your kingdom. May
I heed your word and strive to achieve a
fruitful harvest of caring, kindness and
compassion. I pray for all those who farm
the land and give thanks for the food they
produce.

Amen.

THINK

How can we prepare ourselves to be receptive to the word of God?

COLD WINTER DAYS

He gives snow like wool;
he scatters frost like ashes.

Psalm 147:16

Psalm 147 is a beautiful song of praise to God. It tells us about the things he does to support creation and reminds us to sing his praises.

Sing to the Lord with thanksgiving;
make melody to our God on the lyre.

(verse 7)

As the earth sleeps in winter, it is protected by a blanket of snow until it can awaken to give the new life of spring. This reminds us of God's protection. Both people and nature need to rest, so they can be refreshed, and sleep provides welcome respite from the demands of life. Everything is in balance and we praise God for the wonder of creation. We can trust in his love and know that he will provide for all our needs.

The psalm tells us that God melts the hail, frost and snow with his word, reminding us to take heed and listen.

PRAY

Father in heaven,
I thank you for the beauty of winter when nature sleeps and can wake renewed.
I give thanks for the warmth of home on cold days which reminds me of your love and protection. I pray for those who are homeless. May they find help and support during the cold winter months.
Amen.

THINK

Can you find out about the excellent charities which provide food and shelter for the homeless?

RAINY DAYS

**Ask rain from the Lord
in the season of the spring rain,
from the Lord who makes the storm-clouds,
who gives showers of rain to you,
the vegetation in the field to everyone.**

Zechariah 10:1

REFLECTION

We are reminded that rain comes from God and that he takes care of all our needs. We should pray for rain and for our world, not forgetting to give thanks for God's wonderful creation and for the way that everything works in harmony in order to give life.

We may not be happy to see storm-clouds, but they give us valuable water which helps our crops to grow in the fields.

Sometimes God's plan can be difficult to understand, but like the storm-clouds, it is for the good of all life.

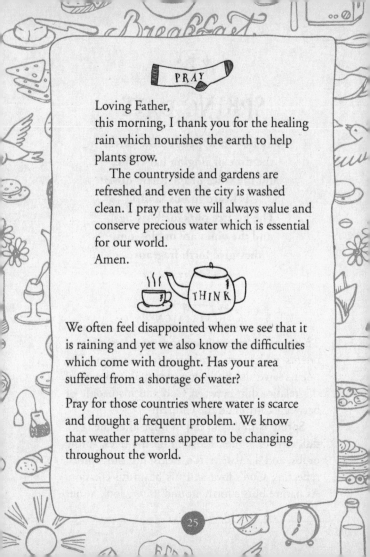

PRAY

Loving Father,
this morning, I thank you for the healing rain which nourishes the earth to help plants grow.

The countryside and gardens are refreshed and even the city is washed clean. I pray that we will always value and conserve precious water which is essential for our world.
Amen.

THINK

We often feel disappointed when we see that it is raining and yet we also know the difficulties which come with drought. Has your area suffered from a shortage of water?

Pray for those countries where water is scarce and drought a frequent problem. We know that weather patterns appear to be changing throughout the world.

SPRING DAYS

**The flowers appear on the earth;
the time of singing has come,
and the voice of the turtle-dove
is heard in our land.
The fig tree puts forth its figs,
and the vines are in blossom;
they give forth fragrance.**

Song of Solomon 2:12, 13

REFLECTION

These words are taken from a series of love poems which are attributed to Solomon. The poems have also been interpreted as a picture of the relationship between God and his people or between Christ and the Church.

Spring is fresh and full of hope after the cold, dull days of winter. Blossom on the trees, spring bulbs and lambs in the fields lift our spirits, reflecting God's love and his beautiful creation. As nature bursts forth around us, we look at our own lives afresh, often with renewed energy as we prepare for spring and summer.

For Christians however, the optimism of the spring season is always mixed with thoughts and preparation for Easter with its mixed emotions.

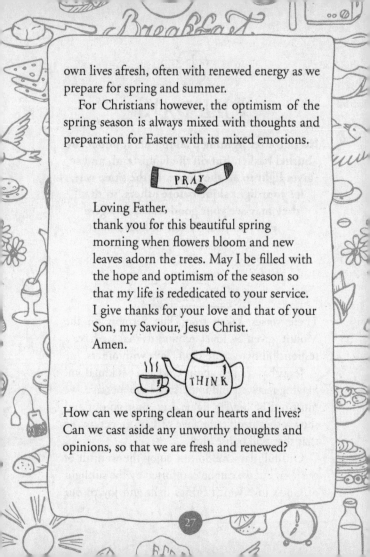

PRAY

Loving Father,
thank you for this beautiful spring
morning when flowers bloom and new
leaves adorn the trees. May I be filled with
the hope and optimism of the season so
that my life is rededicated to your service.
I give thanks for your love and that of your
Son, my Saviour, Jesus Christ.
Amen.

THINK

How can we spring clean our hearts and lives?
Can we cast aside any unworthy thoughts and
opinions, so that we are fresh and renewed?

DULL DAYS

No one after lighting a lamp puts it under the bushel basket, but on the lampstand, and it gives light to all the house. In the same way, let your light shine before others, so that they may see your good works and give glory to your Father in heaven.

Matthew 5:15, 16

REFLECTION

These verses, taken from The Sermon on the Mount, given by Jesus, remind us that we have a responsibility to share God's love with others.

Jesus has spoken about God and his kingdom. Having received and understood the message, we must not be hidden lights, but must go out and show other people the love of God in action, so that they will praise him.

On dull days we do not enjoy the warmth of the sun, but we can be comforted by the sunlight of God's love which brings light and joy to our souls. We are all precious to God and we know that if we share this love with others, we can bring brightness to every day.

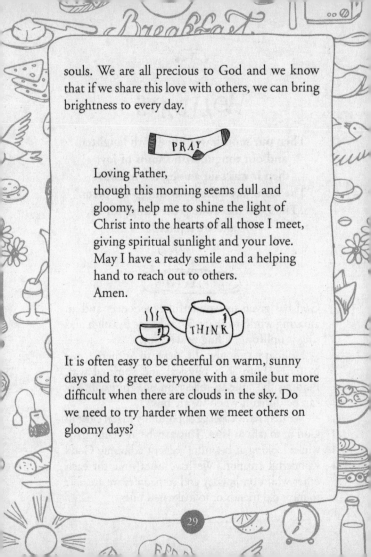

PRAY

Loving Father,
though this morning seems dull and
gloomy, help me to shine the light of
Christ into the hearts of all those I meet,
giving spiritual sunlight and your love.
May I have a ready smile and a helping
hand to reach out to others.
Amen.

THINK

It is often easy to be cheerful on warm, sunny days and to greet everyone with a smile but more difficult when there are clouds in the sky. Do we need to try harder when we meet others on gloomy days?

HOLIDAYS

**Then our mouth was filled with laughter,
and our tongue with shouts of joy;
then it was said among the nations,
'The Lord has done great things for them.'
The Lord has done great things for us,
and we rejoiced.**

Psalm 126:2, 3

REFLECTION

God has given us wonderful experiences and an amazing world to share. The chance to laugh and sing is uplifting, filling us with joy.

Holidays can give us time to recharge our batteries, both in a physical and spiritual way. Finding the time to reflect on our spiritual lives can be difficult when we are busy.

We may have a special opportunity to feel close to God or to talk to Jesus. This may be in a church, or whilst looking at beautiful scenery, admiring God's wonderful creation. We have extra time for each other whilst on holiday and sometimes we are able to meet old friends or to make new ones.

We may hold memories of holidays in our hearts for many years ahead, to be revisited often. These are particularly poignant when people are no longer with us.

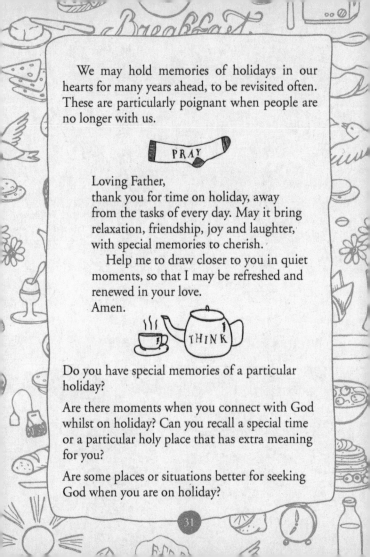

PRAY

Loving Father,
thank you for time on holiday, away
from the tasks of every day. May it bring
relaxation, friendship, joy and laughter,
with special memories to cherish.
   Help me to draw closer to you in quiet
moments, so that I may be refreshed and
renewed in your love.
Amen.

THINK

Do you have special memories of a particular holiday?

Are there moments when you connect with God whilst on holiday? Can you recall a special time or a particular holy place that has extra meaning for you?

Are some places or situations better for seeking God when you are on holiday?

SECTION 2

JESUS

JESUS, MY FRIEND

I do not call you servants any longer, because the servant does not know what the master is doing; but I have called you friends, because I have made known to you everything that I have heard from my Father.

John 15:15

REFLECTION

Jesus is speaking to the disciples, telling them that he has chosen them and is teaching them about God. He is preparing them for the work they will have to do.

In the same way, Jesus tells us about God. He understands us because he lived a human life, experiencing some of the same emotions that we do. He is our friend and reaches out to us, providing a link to God who is beyond our understanding.

Jesus used parables which described earthly situations to explain his teaching. This was not a remote Messiah who was otherworldly but someone who knew about human nature and could explain how to bring people of the earth closer to their God in heaven.

As Christians, we are fortunate that we can talk to Jesus as a friend, knowing that he will understand.

PRAY

Lord Jesus,
thank you for being my friend. I can talk to you, sharing my innermost thoughts and feelings because you know the secrets of my heart. You understand me better than anyone. Help me to walk with you so that I may be a friend to others, showing your love by reaching out where there is need. Amen.

THINK

Do you know someone who needs a friend to talk to today?

Do you have a friend you have not been in contact with for a while? Perhaps a phone call or a message could let them know that you are thinking of them.

BEING A DISCIPLE

Then Jesus said to the Jews who had believed in him, 'If you continue in my word, you are truly my disciples; and you will know the truth, and the truth will make you free.'

John 8:31, 32

REFLECTION

Jesus is telling us that his disciples are not only those he chose to help him, but all those who follow his teaching. This is the good news that we are all disciples of Jesus if we live our lives according to his word and his example.

Jesus speaks about 'the truth' which will lead us to heaven and set us free from sin and the confines of our earthly lives. Knowing about God's kingdom empowers us because Jesus has given us the key. Even after two thousand years, we can still call ourselves disciples and follow Jesus who leads us to the Father.

In John 13:35, Jesus said, 'By this everyone will know that you are my disciples, if you have love for one another.'

When we reach out to others with love in the name of Christ, we show that we are indeed his disciples.

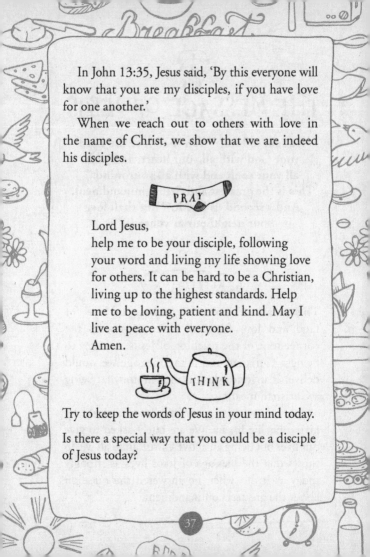

PRAY

Lord Jesus,
help me to be your disciple, following
your word and living my life showing love
for others. It can be hard to be a Christian,
living up to the highest standards. Help
me to be loving, patient and kind. May I
live at peace with everyone.
Amen.

THINK

Try to keep the words of Jesus in your mind today.

Is there a special way that you could be a disciple of Jesus today?

THE MESSAGE OF JESUS

**He said to him, '"You shall love the Lord
your God with all your heart, and with
all your soul, and with all your mind."
This is the greatest and first commandment.
And a second is like it: "You shall love
your neighbour as yourself."'**

Matthew 22:37-39

REFLECTION

This great and powerful message of love for
God and love for each other represents the
cornerstone of the teaching of Jesus. It is key to
being a Christian and is the message we would
deliver if anyone asked us to sum up what being
a Christian means.

Jesus showed his great love for the world by
giving his life for us. We are rarely asked to give
our lives but being an active Christian in all we do
shows that the message of Jesus lives as strongly
today as it did when he answered the question
about the greatest commandment.

Jesus added the second commandment to show how we can put God's love into practice in our lives. By showing love to others, we show God's love.

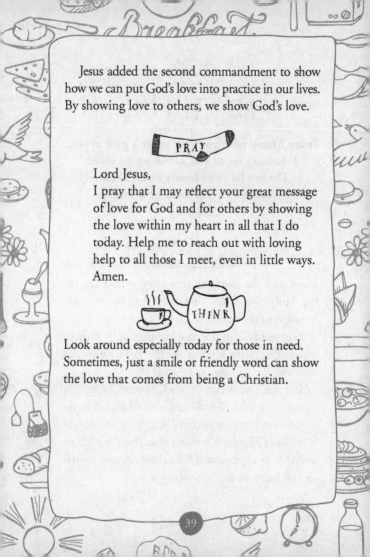

PRAY

Lord Jesus,
I pray that I may reflect your great message of love for God and for others by showing the love within my heart in all that I do today. Help me to reach out with loving help to all those I meet, even in little ways. Amen.

THINK

Look around especially today for those in need. Sometimes, just a smile or friendly word can show the love that comes from being a Christian.

BE WITH ME

Peace I leave with you; my peace I give to you.
I do not give to you as the world gives.
Do not let your hearts be troubled,
and do not let them be afraid.

John 14:27

REFLECTION

Jesus told the disciples that they would receive the Holy Spirit and that they should carry his message to the world.

His words of peace and comfort stay with us today, along with his promise that if we follow his teaching, he will always be with us.

It is not always easy to be a Christian, especially in today's world. We all experience difficult times in our lives and sometimes it is hard to see the way ahead clearly. Knowing that Jesus is with us and that he experienced life's challenges, comforts us and helps us to have courage.

And remember, I am with you always,
to the end of the age.

(Matthew 28:20)

PRAY

Lord Jesus,
I am comforted because I know that you
are with me through every day whatever
happens. You give me strength and peace
so that I can carry on even when life is hard.
May I place you at the heart of all that I
do, knowing that through the certainty
of your love, I can face whatever life may
bring.
Amen.

THINK

Have you been through a time when your faith
in Jesus gave you particular comfort?

Conversely, have you experienced a time when
you felt it was hard to be a Christian? If so, think
about how you emerged from this time and why
your faith is important today.

CALM

He woke up and rebuked the wind, and said to the sea, 'Peace! Be still!' Then the wind ceased, and there was a dead calm.

Mark 4:39

REFLECTION

The disciples believed that they were going to die when the boat filled with water in a great storm on the Sea of Galilee. Jesus was asleep, and they woke him, saying, 'Teacher, do you not care that we are perishing?' (verse 38).

When Jesus had calmed the storm, he asked them why they were frightened, saying, 'Have you still no faith?' (verse 40).

Faith was important to Jesus and trust in him brings us calm in our daily lives because we do believe and know that he is always with us and part of everything we do. Jesus said that those who had not seen him and yet believed, were truly blessed *(see Ascension Reflection)*.

PRAY

Lord Jesus,
my soul is troubled with earthly worries.
Please still my heart as you calmed the
storm. I place my trust in you, knowing
that your peaceful love surrounds me
always and I can face each day knowing
that you are by my side.
Amen.

THINK

We all experience our own life storms. Can you
think of particular times when Jesus has brought
you calm and comfort?

A BEACON OF LIGHT

**Again Jesus spoke to them, saying,
'I am the light of the world. Whoever
follows me will never walk in darkness
but will have the light of life.'**

John 8:12

The words of Jesus remind us that he is the light, leading us out of the darkness of ignorance into the light of God's love.

The Saviour links us to God and guides us to the Father if we follow him. By focusing on the light of Christ, we can grow in love and obedience to God, turning from the darkness of wrongdoing towards the light and love of goodness within our lives.

We may not always get things right but by concentrating on the Christ light, we can persevere and will move in the right direction: towards God.

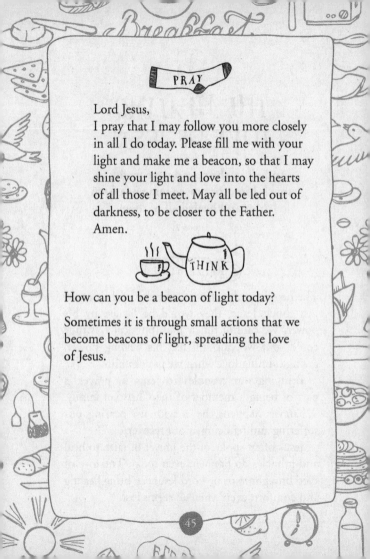

PRAY

Lord Jesus,
I pray that I may follow you more closely
in all I do today. Please fill me with your
light and make me a beacon, so that I may
shine your light and love into the hearts
of all those I meet. May all be led out of
darkness, to be closer to the Father.
Amen.

THINK

How can you be a beacon of light today?

Sometimes it is through small actions that we
become beacons of light, spreading the love
of Jesus.

THE HEALING LOVE OF JESUS

And all in the crowd were trying to touch him, for power came out from him and healed all of them.

Luke 6:19

REFLECTION

The people in the crowd knew that if they could just touch Jesus, they would be healed by his power. We cannot touch Jesus physically as they could, but we can still feel his healing power, giving calming love when we pray to him.

Bringing our troubles to Jesus in prayer is part of being a member of the Christian family. Whatever happens, he is with us, bearing our suffering and rejoicing at our recovery.

Jesus often spoke of the power of faith to heal and miracles do happen, even today. The love of God brought to us by Lord Jesus can bring healing and comfort, even when all seems lost.

We can pray quietly at home, or with others. Many churches have healing services and laying on of hands to help those who are unwell. Where recovery is not expected, the peaceful atmosphere found in hospices shows the value of calm, loving preparation for the end of life's journey. This is helped by faith and prayer, both for the person who is dying and for those left behind.

PRAY

Lord Jesus,
I thank you for your healing love which fills me with peacefulness. When I am suffering or afraid, you are with me, bringing hope and even joy to be alive. You hear my prayers for those close to me and I know that you will surround them with your love.
Amen.

THINK

Do you know someone in need of healing love today?

BEING BUSY

But the Lord answered her, 'Martha, Martha, you are worried and distracted by many things; there is need of only one thing. Mary has chosen the better part, which will not be taken away from her.'

Luke 10:41, 42

REFLECTION

Jesus is telling Martha that she is so worried about daily tasks and little things, that she has missed the importance of hearing his words. Although Mary has not helped Martha with her tasks, she has stopped to listen to Jesus.

This story resonates so much with many of us when we struggle to do everything from day to day. It also reflects the challenges of fast-paced, modern life. Jesus is giving us permission to take some time off so that we can see the bigger picture. Some things are important, but we can miss them because we are too busy.

When we rush around, we forget to take time to be still and to connect with God. Perhaps quietly at home, or in a garden or park if not in a church, we can pause for a few moments to remember the words of Jesus.

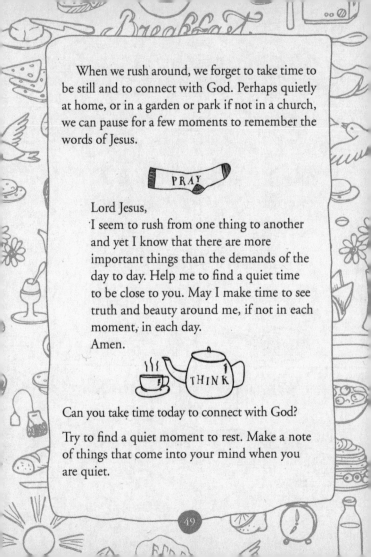

PRAY

Lord Jesus,
I seem to rush from one thing to another and yet I know that there are more important things than the demands of the day to day. Help me to find a quiet time to be close to you. May I make time to see truth and beauty around me, if not in each moment, in each day.
Amen.

THINK

Can you take time today to connect with God?

Try to find a quiet moment to rest. Make a note of things that come into your mind when you are quiet.

SECTION
3

COMMUNITIES

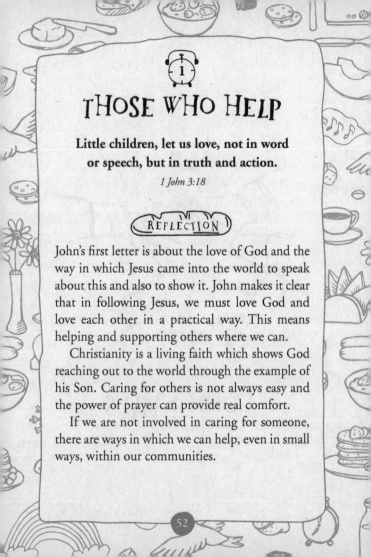

THOSE WHO HELP

Little children, let us love, not in word or speech, but in truth and action.

1 John 3:18

REFLECTION

John's first letter is about the love of God and the way in which Jesus came into the world to speak about this and also to show it. John makes it clear that in following Jesus, we must love God and love each other in a practical way. This means helping and supporting others where we can.

Christianity is a living faith which shows God reaching out to the world through the example of his Son. Caring for others is not always easy and the power of prayer can provide real comfort.

If we are not involved in caring for someone, there are ways in which we can help, even in small ways, within our communities.

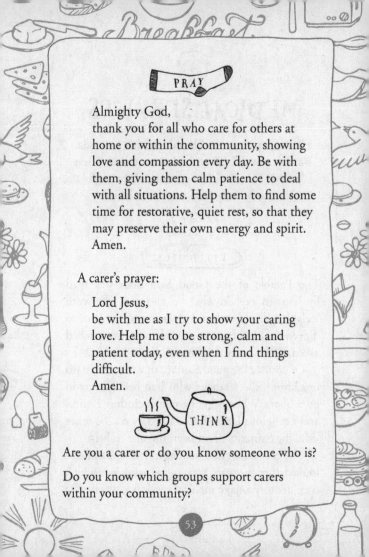

PRAY

Almighty God,
thank you for all who care for others at home or within the community, showing love and compassion every day. Be with them, giving them calm patience to deal with all situations. Help them to find some time for restorative, quiet rest, so that they may preserve their own energy and spirit.
Amen.

A carer's prayer:

Lord Jesus,
be with me as I try to show your caring love. Help me to be strong, calm and patient today, even when I find things difficult.
Amen.

THINK

Are you a carer or do you know someone who is?

Do you know which groups support carers within your community?

MEDICAL SERVICES

**He went to him and bandaged his wounds,
having poured oil and wine on them. Then
he put him on his own animal, brought
him to an inn, and took care of him.**

Luke 10:34

The Parable of the Good Samaritan was used
by Jesus to explain what he meant by the word
'neighbour'. He had told a teacher of the Law, to
'Love your neighbour as yourself' and the man had
asked, 'Who is my neighbour?' (Luke 10:27, 29).

Of course, the good Samaritan was good to his
neighbour, the stranger who had been set upon
by robbers. When other people, including a priest
and a religious Levite had walked by on the other
side, the Samaritan had been the one to help.

The Samaritan had bandaged the wounds and
looked after the man, showing a caring love which
is evident in today's medical services, as well as in

other caring roles. People who dedicate their lives to the welfare of others hold a special place within our communities.

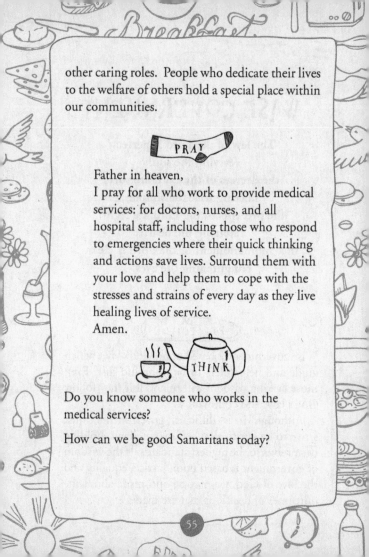

PRAY

Father in heaven,
I pray for all who work to provide medical services: for doctors, nurses, and all hospital staff, including those who respond to emergencies where their quick thinking and actions save lives. Surround them with your love and help them to cope with the stresses and strains of every day as they live healing lives of service.
Amen.

THINK

Do you know someone who works in the medical services?

How can we be good Samaritans today?

WISE GOVERNMENT

**The law of the Lord is perfect;
reviving the soul;
the decrees of the Lord are sure,
making wise the simple;
the precepts of the Lord are right,
rejoicing the heart;
the commandment of the Lord is clear,
enlightening the eyes.**

Psalm 19:7, 8

REFLECTION

Wise government is based upon God's laws which guide and help rulers to be right and just. Even those lacking wisdom will rule well if they follow God's laws and commands.

Although it is difficult, governments must strive to be fair to all when making laws, holding themselves to the highest standards. If the wisdom of government is based upon justice, equality and the love of God, we may be optimistic about the outcomes of decisions that are made.

God sent his Son to show us the way forward:

For a child has been born for us,
a son given to us;
authority rests upon his shoulders;
and he is named
Wonderful Counsellor, Mighty God,
Everlasting Father, Prince of Peace.

Isaiah 9:6

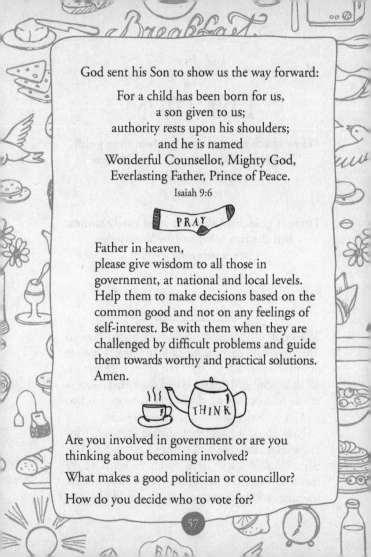

PRAY

Father in heaven,
please give wisdom to all those in
government, at national and local levels.
Help them to make decisions based on the
common good and not on any feelings of
self-interest. Be with them when they are
challenged by difficult problems and guide
them towards worthy and practical solutions.
Amen.

THINK

Are you involved in government or are you
thinking about becoming involved?

What makes a good politician or councillor?

How do you decide who to vote for?

EDUCATION

**How much better to get wisdom than gold!
To get understanding is to be chosen
rather than silver.**

Proverbs 16:16

**There is gold, and abundance of costly stones;
but the lips informed by knowledge
are a precious jewel.**

Proverbs 20:15

The book of Proverbs gives advice about how to live and speaks of the value of knowledge. It points out that reverence for the Lord is the cornerstone of all teaching. Having established that God is at the heart of all we do, we must work hard to achieve knowledge and ultimately wisdom.

Nowadays, we understand that the search for knowledge does not end when we leave full-time education. We still have much to learn as we travel through life and our lives are enriched by learning, whatever our age. As the world changes, the willingness to keep learning helps us to manage our daily lives and also to feel more connected to the society around us.

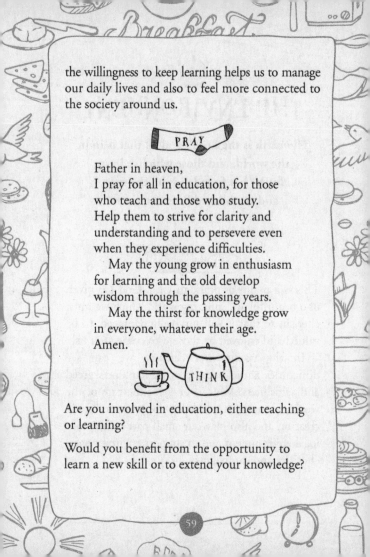

PRAY

Father in heaven,
I pray for all in education, for those
who teach and those who study.
Help them to strive for clarity and
understanding and to persevere even
when they experience difficulties.
May the young grow in enthusiasm
for learning and the old develop
wisdom through the passing years.
May the thirst for knowledge grow
in everyone, whatever their age.
Amen.

THINK

Are you involved in education, either teaching or learning?

Would you benefit from the opportunity to learn a new skill or to extend your knowledge?

THE ENVIRONMENT

**The earth is the Lord's and all that is in it,
the world, and those who live in it;
for he has founded it on the seas,
and established it on the rivers.**

Psalm 24:1, 2

This is a psalm of praise to God. God has given us a beautiful and amazing world which we must cherish, so that it will survive undamaged, to be valued and enjoyed by those who come after us.

In the twenty-first century, we can see difficulties ahead because of humankind's greed and selfishness. We can pray for the care of the world around us in order to preserve God's creation and also play our small part to help our local environment and to support environmental charities and campaigns.

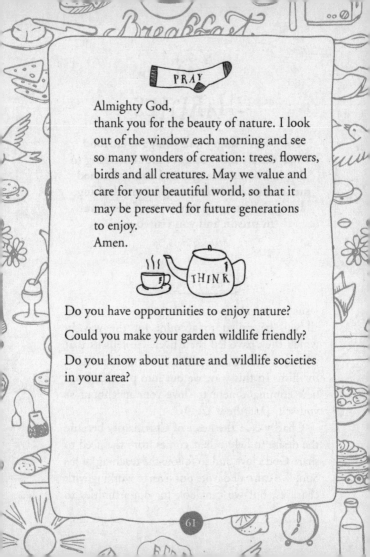

PRAY

Almighty God,
thank you for the beauty of nature. I look
out of the window each morning and see
so many wonders of creation: trees, flowers,
birds and all creatures. May we value and
care for your beautiful world, so that it
may be preserved for future generations
to enjoy.
Amen.

THINK

Do you have opportunities to enjoy nature?

Could you make your garden wildlife friendly?

Do you know about nature and wildlife societies
in your area?

CHARITIES

'For I was hungry and you gave me food,
I was thirsty and you gave me something to
drink, I was a stranger and you welcomed
me, I was naked and you gave me clothing,
I was sick and you took care of me, I was
in prison and you visited me.'

Matthew 25:35, 36

REFLECTION

Jesus is speaking of Judgement Day, when
all will be called to account for the way in
which they have led their lives. He tells us that
whenever we do something for others, we do it
for him. In this way, we put into practice Jesus'
new commandment to 'love your neighbour as
yourself' (Matthew 22:39).

Charity is at the heart of Christianity because
the desire to help others comes from the need to
share God's love and to follow the teaching of his
Son. We can't all devote our lives to working with
charities, but we can look for opportunities to

help whenever we are able to. Even small acts of charity can make a difference and help to make our society a better one.

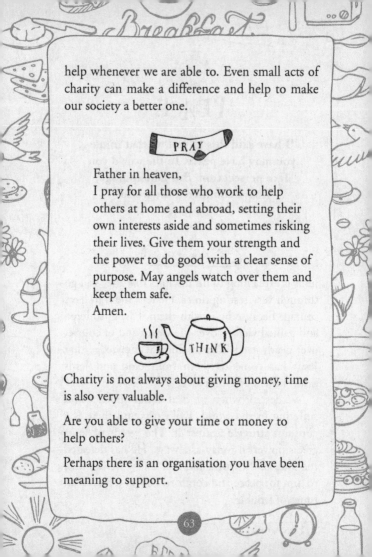

PRAY

Father in heaven,
I pray for all those who work to help others at home and abroad, setting their own interests aside and sometimes risking their lives. Give them your strength and the power to do good with a clear sense of purpose. May angels watch over them and keep them safe.
Amen.

THINK

Charity is not always about giving money, time is also very valuable.

Are you able to give your time or money to help others?

Perhaps there is an organisation you have been meaning to support.

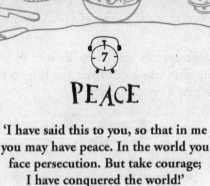

PEACE

**'I have said this to you, so that in me
you may have peace. In the world you
face persecution. But take courage;
I have conquered the world!'**

John 16:33

REFLECTION

Jesus is explaining to his disciples that they will go
through very testing times. He tells them to have
courage because he is with them, having suffered
and gained victory over the world and of course,
over death itself. The disciples acknowledge that
Jesus has come to them from God and Jesus
assures them of God's love.

We despair when we hear about violence and
suffering in the world. Evil exists and there is a
constant struggle against it. The words of Jesus
are as powerful today as always. He has defeated
the trials of the world and that is why we can turn
to him for peace and comfort, now and forever in
times of trouble.

Prayer is very powerful and every prayer for peace helps our troubled world. We can pray for peace and the calming love of Christ to prevail.

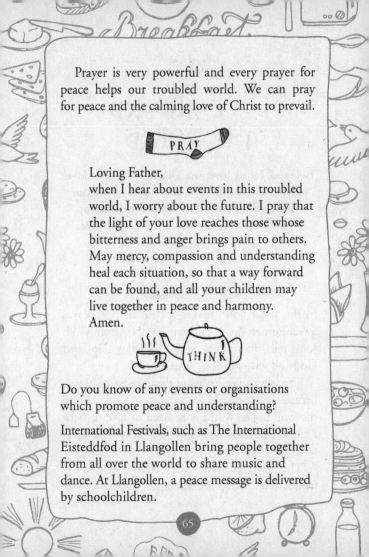

PRAY

Loving Father,
when I hear about events in this troubled world, I worry about the future. I pray that the light of your love reaches those whose bitterness and anger brings pain to others. May mercy, compassion and understanding heal each situation, so that a way forward can be found, and all your children may live together in peace and harmony.
Amen.

THINK

Do you know of any events or organisations which promote peace and understanding?

International Festivals, such as The International Eisteddfod in Llangollen bring people together from all over the world to share music and dance. At Llangollen, a peace message is delivered by schoolchildren.

LOVE AROUND THE WORLD

Beloved, let us love one another, because love is from God; everyone who loves is born of God and knows God. Whoever does not love does not know God, for God is love.

1 John 4:7, 8

REFLECTION

In this letter, John makes it clear that Jesus was a real human being but that he came from God. John tells his readers to live in fellowship with God and with his Son, Jesus Christ.

The letter says a lot about the importance of love because Jesus brought the message of God's love to the world. The world is in need of love to fight against evil and to bring peace and fellowship to all.

The power of prayer can send love around the world, reinforcing the message brought by our

Saviour. When we send the love and light of Christ out into the world, we help the power of God's love to grow, so that dark thoughts and deeds may be vanquished.

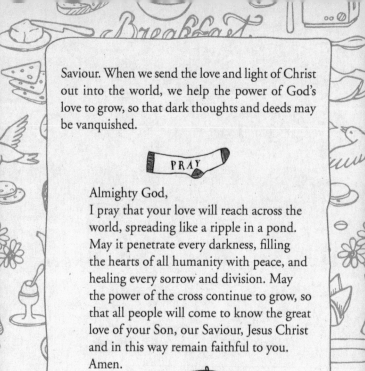

PRAY

Almighty God,
I pray that your love will reach across the world, spreading like a ripple in a pond. May it penetrate every darkness, filling the hearts of all humanity with peace, and healing every sorrow and division. May the power of the cross continue to grow, so that all people will come to know the great love of your Son, our Saviour, Jesus Christ and in this way remain faithful to you. Amen.

THINK

Can you send your love around the world, starting where you live and imagining it spreading across the country and reaching all nations?

SECTION
4

HELP AND SUPPORT

FORGIVENESS

**Then Peter came and said to him,
'Lord, if another member of the church
sins against me, how often should
I forgive? As many as seven times?'
Jesus said to him, 'Not seven times,
but I tell you, seventy-seven times.'**

Matthew 18:21, 22

REFLECTION

Jesus is telling Peter and us, that there is no limit
to how many times we should forgive each other
because God forgives us. He goes on to tell the
Parable of the Unforgiving Servant.

In the story, the king did not cancel the debt of
his servant because the man had refused to do the
same for a fellow servant who owed him money.
The message is clear, we must truly forgive others
from within our hearts, so that God may also
forgive us.

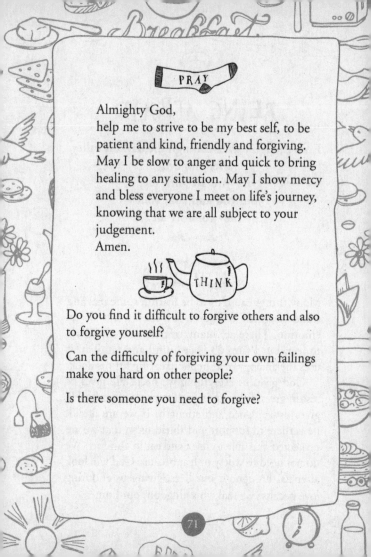

PRAY

Almighty God,
help me to strive to be my best self, to be
patient and kind, friendly and forgiving.
May I be slow to anger and quick to bring
healing to any situation. May I show mercy
and bless everyone I meet on life's journey,
knowing that we are all subject to your
judgement.
Amen.

THINK

Do you find it difficult to forgive others and also
to forgive yourself?

Can the difficulty of forgiving your own failings
make you hard on other people?

Is there someone you need to forgive?

BEING AFRAID

Even though I walk through the darkest valley,
I fear no evil;
for you are with me;
your rod and your staff –
they comfort me.

Psalm 23:4

REFLECTION

Many things cause us to be fearful, some real and some imagined. However, fear itself is a very real emotion. There are many references in the Bible to fear, but Psalm 23 is beautiful and familiar. It uses the analogy of a shepherd caring for his flock.

God gives us everything we need. He gives us rest in green fields and by quiet pools of water. He gives us guidance and strength. If we are afraid, he is there to support and shield us so that we are protected and able to relax and eat in comfort. We do not need to worry or fear because God will look after us throughout our lives, giving us enduring love because we make his kingdom our home.

Also read Psalm 34, which tells us how God looks after the righteous: 'I sought the Lord, and he answered me, and delivered me from all my fears' (Psalm 34:4).

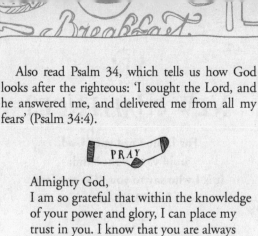

PRAY

Almighty God,
I am so grateful that within the knowledge of your power and glory, I can place my trust in you. I know that you are always with me, helping me to find a way through troubled times. You give me the strength to move forward, so that I can face every fear and challenge because I am certain of your supporting love.
Amen.

THINK

Psalms 23 and 34, are very empowering and comforting if you feel afraid.

Singing hymns can also be comforting in some situations, giving confidence and driving out fearful thoughts.

Is there someone you can talk to if you are worried?

NEW CHALLENGES

For I, the Lord your God,
hold your right hand;
it is I who say to you, 'Do not fear,
I will help you.'

Isaiah 41:13

REFLECTION

The message given by God to the prophet Isaiah promised that the people who were in exile in Babylon would be set free and taken home to Jerusalem. God would give them the strength to overcome their fears and meet their needs.

If we trust in God, we need not fear new challenges. Even if we appear to be weak, he will help us to find the way forward.

Life is full of changing situations, new opportunities and challenges. Sometimes we wonder if we can cope with the unfamiliar and it is tempting to cling to the things that we know best. Gradually, in time, everything becomes familiar again and we increase in confidence. Prayer can help us to make this transition in a more positive and supported way.

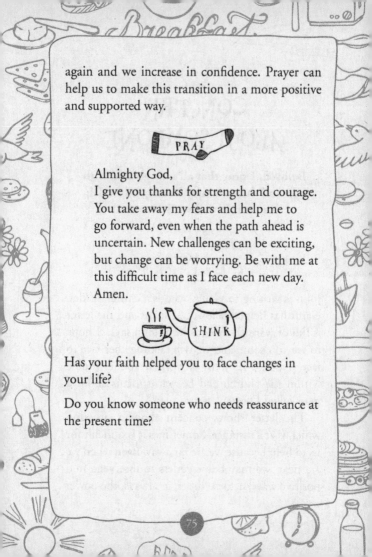

PRAY

Almighty God,
I give you thanks for strength and courage. You take away my fears and help me to go forward, even when the path ahead is uncertain. New challenges can be exciting, but change can be worrying. Be with me at this difficult time as I face each new day. Amen.

THINK

Has your faith helped you to face changes in your life?

Do you know someone who needs reassurance at the present time?

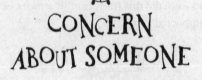

CONCERN ABOUT SOMEONE

Beloved, I pray that all may go well with you and that you may be in good health, just as it is well with your soul.

3 John, verse 2

REFLECTION

John is writing to Gaius, who is a church leader. Gaius has helped fellow Christians and the letter is full of warmth towards him. John says, 'I hope to see you soon, and we will talk together face to face' (verse 14). John is worried about trouble within the church and he warns Gaius about a man called Diotrephes.

The letter shows concern about a situation which is at a distance. Sometimes it is difficult for us to help because we are far away. Even when we are near, we may be powerless to intervene in a positive way. At these times, as always, the power of prayer is particularly important. Concern can be about events, when we cannot change the circumstances, or perhaps a person's health, when we can only watch and wait for news. God holds us all in his hands and knows what is best for us.

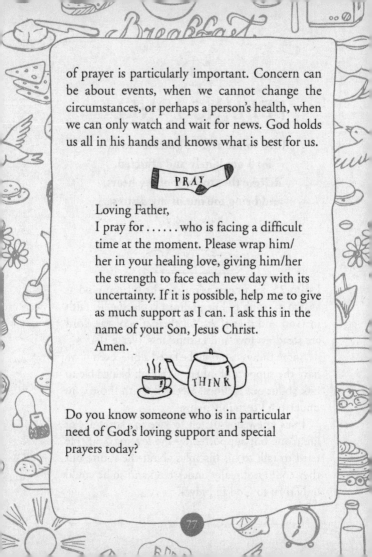

Loving Father,
I pray for . . . . . . who is facing a difficult time at the moment. Please wrap him/her in your healing love, giving him/her the strength to face each new day with its uncertainty. If it is possible, help me to give as much support as I can. I ask this in the name of your Son, Jesus Christ.
Amen.

Do you know someone who is in particular need of God's loving support and special prayers today?

FEELING LONELY

Turn to me and be gracious to me,
for I am lonely and afflicted.
Relieve the troubles of my heart,
and bring me out of my distress.

Psalm 25:16, 17

REFLECTION

Psalm 25 is a prayer asking for help from God at a time of trouble. The psalmist is placing his faith in God and says that, 'All the paths of the Lord are steadfast love and faithfulness' (verse 10).

Some things can only be faced alone, even if we have the support of others, although being able to talk about our feelings, especially with those who understand certainly helps.

Jesus knew how it felt to face the struggles of life alone but supported by the love of God. He tried to talk to his disciples about the future but they could not really understand and so he could only turn to God in prayer.

When we feel alone, we can pray to the Father, or to the Lord Jesus, for help or guidance and to enable us to go forward, confident in steadfast and supporting love.

PRAY

Lord Jesus,
I feel so alone. I pray to you, knowing that you hear me and that you are always with me. Guide me as I step into the unknown, bewildered, but trusting in your strength and in the love and mercy of the Father. Amen.

THINK

We all experience times when we feel alone and yet help can be at hand if we are willing to accept it.

Sometimes, others are feeling the same way and would welcome a message or call.

Volunteering or taking up a hobby can be a good way to meet like-minded people.

SAFE TRAVEL

**The Lord will keep you from all evil;
he will keep your life.
The Lord will keep
your going out and your coming in
from this time on and for evermore.**

Psalm 121:7, 8

REFLECTION

Psalm 121 is a wonderful prayer of praise for the
Lord, our Protector.

> I lift up my eyes to the hills –
> from where will my help come?
> My help comes from the Lord,
> who made heaven and earth.
>
> (verses 1, 2)

Journeys today are often a challenge, with busy
roads, trains and planes. Preparing calmly and
leaving in good time can help a great deal, making a
big difference to safety, enjoyment and punctuality.

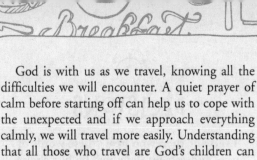

God is with us as we travel, knowing all the difficulties we will encounter. A quiet prayer of calm before starting off can help us to cope with the unexpected and if we approach everything calmly, we will travel more easily. Understanding that all those who travel are God's children can help us to manage delays and difficulties.

PRAY

Father in heaven,
be with me today as I face a journey. Help me to be calm and cheerful, even if it is busy and difficult. May I be helpful to those I meet, knowing that they too find travel a challenge. I pray that I may arrive safely at my destination, praising you, my Protector. Amen.

THINK

Have you planned a stop for rest and refreshment on your journey?

Are you able to allow extra time for your journey?

How did people prepare for journeys in Bible times?

DECISIONS

**'Everyone then who hears these words of
mine and acts on them will be like a wise
man who built his house on rock. The rain
fell, the floods came, and the winds blew
and beat on that house, but it did not fall,
because it had been founded on rock.'**

Matthew 7:24, 25

REFLECTION

Jesus gives a parable with a clear meaning when
he compares the men who built their houses on
rock or sand. In order to make the right decisions,
we must take notice of his teaching, so that what
we do is based upon truth and love. We all strive
to be like the man who built on rock but fear that
there are times when we build on sand.

Praying for help with our decisions can help
us to find the right way forward, especially when
the choices are difficult, or the facts unclear. As
Christians, we try to consider the needs of others
in all decisions that we make.

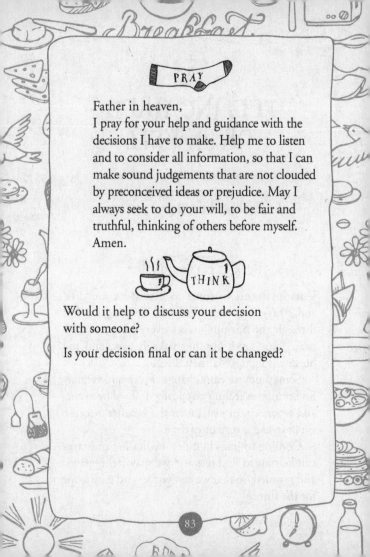

PRAY

Father in heaven,
I pray for your help and guidance with the
decisions I have to make. Help me to listen
and to consider all information, so that I can
make sound judgements that are not clouded
by preconceived ideas or prejudice. May I
always seek to do your will, to be fair and
truthful, thinking of others before myself.
Amen.

THINK

Would it help to discuss your decision
with someone?

Is your decision final or can it be changed?

FEELING TIRED OR UNWELL

**'Come to me, all you that are
weary and are carrying heavy
burdens, and I will give you rest.'**

Matthew 11:28

REFLECTION

Jesus invites us to come to him if we are tired and struggling with life's path. Trusting in God through the Saviour makes everything easier to bear. Jesus says: 'For my yoke is easy, and my burden is light' (Matthew 11:30).

Sometimes we can't change things and we may find ourselves feeling physically drained by events and emotions, or just 'under the weather' because we have had a very busy time.

Coming to Jesus in quiet meditation or prayer can help us to find rest and we may feel renewed and restored, so that we can go forward with hope for the future.

The light of Christ is uplifting, helping us to feel brighter and more hopeful, even when we have been weighed down by tiredness and ill health.

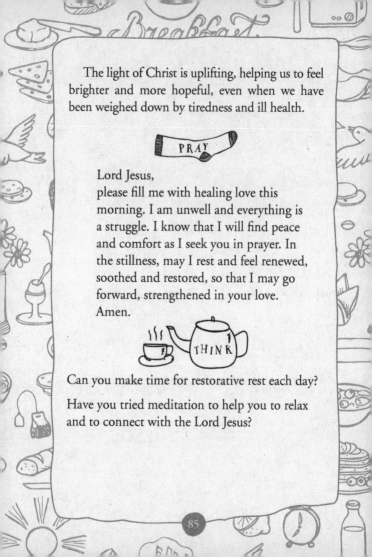

PRAY

Lord Jesus,
please fill me with healing love this morning. I am unwell and everything is a struggle. I know that I will find peace and comfort as I seek you in prayer. In the stillness, may I rest and feel renewed, soothed and restored, so that I may go forward, strengthened in your love.
Amen.

THINK

Can you make time for restorative rest each day?

Have you tried meditation to help you to relax and to connect with the Lord Jesus?

SECTION 5

FESTIVALS

ADVENT

The angel said to her, 'The Holy Spirit will come upon you, and the power of the Most High will overshadow you; therefore the child to be born will be holy; he will be called Son of God.'

Luke 1:35

REFLECTION

During Advent, we anticipate the Nativity of Jesus and think about the events leading up to his birth in Bethlehem.

We begin with the annunciation, when the angel told Mary that she had been chosen to be the mother of God's Son.

Mary replied to the angel, 'Here am I, the servant of the Lord; let it be with me according to your word' (Luke 1:38).

An angel also appeared to Joseph in a dream, telling him that the baby was conceived by the power of the Holy Spirit and to name the baby Jesus.

This is a time to consider how Mary and Joseph coped with the enormity of the news, especially within their culture, and how they made preparations for the birth of Jesus.

Of course, we also prepare to welcome baby Jesus within our hearts once more, as we approach the Christmas season.

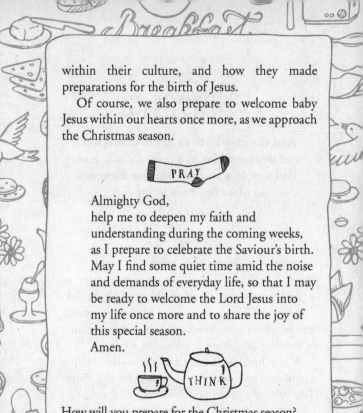

PRAY

Almighty God,
help me to deepen my faith and
understanding during the coming weeks,
as I prepare to celebrate the Saviour's birth.
May I find some quiet time amid the noise
and demands of everyday life, so that I may
be ready to welcome the Lord Jesus into
my life once more and to share the joy of
this special season.
Amen.

THINK

How will you prepare for the Christmas season?

Will you take time to think about coming of the Saviour's birth?

Are you preparing for a Christmas with Christ at its heart?

CHRISTMAS

**And she gave birth to her firstborn son
and wrapped him in bands of cloth, and
laid him in a manger, because there was
no place for them in the inn.**

Luke 2:7

Every Christmas brings a new opportunity to experience the wonder of the birth of God's Son. The Christ Child gives renewed hope to the world, that people may be drawn together in peace because of the tiny baby, born in a humble stable.

A star heralds 'the light of the world', calling shepherds and wise men to witness the birth. The light of the Christ Child reaches the darkest corners of the world with love for humankind and burns brightly within our hearts, as we celebrate God's love for each one of us, shown by the gift of his Son.

'To you is born this day in the city of David a Saviour, who is the Messiah, the Lord' (Luke

2:11). Although the story is so familiar, its magic reaches us anew and we are uplifted with the joy of the Saviour's birth once again.

PRAY

Almighty God,
kneeling at the stable on this special morning, I give you thanks for the gift of your Son and pray that the coming of the Christ Child will give the world hope for a brighter, more peaceful future.

May the Light of the World shine into my mind and the flame of love burn brightly within my heart, helping me to draw closer to you and to my Saviour. Amen.

THINK

What are your wishes for the coming year?

What are your hopes for the world in the new year?

LENT

**And the Spirit immediately drove him
out into the wilderness. He was in the
wilderness for forty days, tempted by
Satan; and he was with the wild beasts;
and the angels waited on him.**

Mark 1:12, 13

REFLECTION

Jesus went into the wilderness to be alone, to
pray and to prepare himself for his ministry and
the ordeal which he knew was to come. He put
himself to the test, to make sure that he was able
to carry out the task before him, facing every
weakness and challenging himself to find ways
of withstanding the suffering he knew he would
have to endure.

We are not asked to go out into the wilderness to
face such an ordeal, but we can ask God to forgive
us for things we have done wrong and also examine
our lives to see if we can become better Christians.
In this way, we prepare ourselves for Eastertide.

Traditionally, people celebrated on Shrove Tuesday (the day before Ash Wednesday) before fasting during Lent.

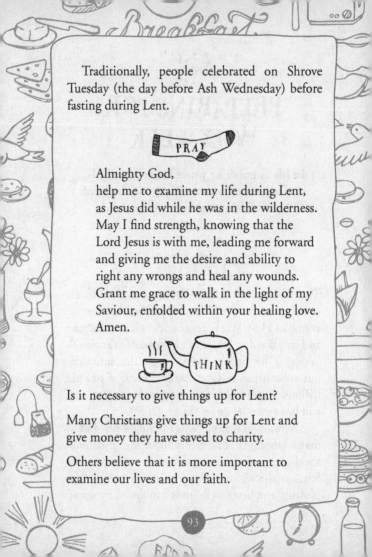

PRAY

Almighty God,
help me to examine my life during Lent,
as Jesus did while he was in the wilderness.
May I find strength, knowing that the
Lord Jesus is with me, leading me forward
and giving me the desire and ability to
right any wrongs and heal any wounds.
Grant me grace to walk in the light of my
Saviour, enfolded within your healing love.
Amen.

THINK

Is it necessary to give things up for Lent?

Many Christians give things up for Lent and give money they have saved to charity.

Others believe that it is more important to examine our lives and our faith.

PREPARING FOR HOLY WEEK

In his anguish he prayed more earnestly, and his sweat became like great drops of blood falling down on the ground.

Luke 22:44

REFLECTION

This verse from Luke shows us how difficult it was even for Jesus to prepare for the horrific events of Holy Week. Jesus knew what was ahead and he prayed to his Father in heaven 'in anguish', asking if he had to go through the suffering, but submitting to God's will: 'Father, if you are willing, remove this cup from me; yet, not my will but yours be done' (Luke 22:42).

There are so many events in Holy Week and so many emotions. The triumph of the 'hosannas' amid the entry into Jerusalem, the anger felt by Jesus at the money-changers in the temple, the plotting and betrayal by Judas, followed by arrest, trial, crucifixion and then, at last, resurrection, bring a wave of changing emotions.

Through it all, the suffering of Jesus remains uppermost in our minds, and our own feelings and reactions do not become easier with the passing years. A quiet time of prayer or meditation gives us the chance to prepare ourselves for this most significant week.

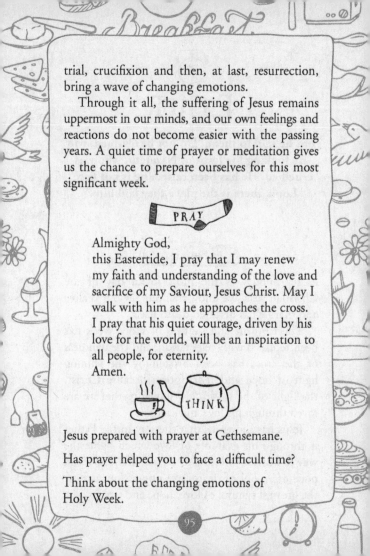

PRAY

Almighty God,
this Eastertide, I pray that I may renew
my faith and understanding of the love and
sacrifice of my Saviour, Jesus Christ. May I
walk with him as he approaches the cross.
I pray that his quiet courage, driven by his
love for the world, will be an inspiration to
all people, for eternity.
Amen.

THINK

Jesus prepared with prayer at Gethsemane.

Has prayer helped you to face a difficult time?

Think about the changing emotions of
Holy Week.

EASTER

But he said to them, 'Do not be alarmed; you are looking for Jesus of Nazareth, who was crucified. He has been raised; he is not here. Look, there is the place they laid him.'

Mark 16:6

REFLECTION

Easter Sunday is the most joyful day of the Christian year. We know that our Saviour is alive and that he has defeated death itself.

The torment and sadness of Holy Week has been replaced with celebration, and the darkness of the cross has been broken by the shining light of hope and redemption because Christ, the light of the world, has shown us that we are saved through his love and sacrifice.

Jesus has shown us that the way to the Father is through his example of love which lights the way to heaven, granting us eternal life. The cross, once a symbol of death and oppression, is now the greatest symbol of love, hope and peace.

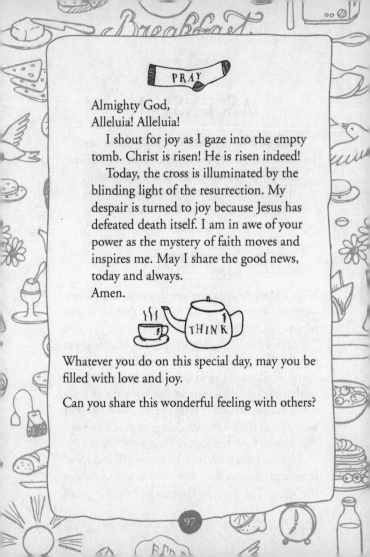

PRAY

Almighty God,
Alleluia! Alleluia!

I shout for joy as I gaze into the empty tomb. Christ is risen! He is risen indeed!

Today, the cross is illuminated by the blinding light of the resurrection. My despair is turned to joy because Jesus has defeated death itself. I am in awe of your power as the mystery of faith moves and inspires me. May I share the good news, today and always.

Amen.

THINK

Whatever you do on this special day, may you be filled with love and joy.

Can you share this wonderful feeling with others?

ASCENSION

Jesus said to her, 'Do not hold on to me, because I have not yet ascended to the Father. But go to my brothers and say to them. "I am ascending to my Father and your Father, to my God and your God."'

John 20:17

REFLECTION

When Mary Magdalene saw Jesus in the garden near the empty tomb, he told her that he would return to God, his Father.

Later, after being with the disciples for some time, Jesus explained about the gift of the Holy Spirit. God would send the Holy Spirit to them, so that they could continue the ministry of Jesus when he was no longer with them: 'When he had said this, as they were watching, he was lifted up, and a cloud took him out of their sight' (Acts 1:9).

The disciples went back to Jerusalem and spent time in prayer, so that they were ready to receive the Spirit. The disciple Thomas had needed proof of the nail marks and spear wound in order to accept that Jesus had survived death. Jesus said to him, 'Have you believed because you have seen me? Blessed are those who have not seen and yet have come to believe' (John 20:29).

Christians today can take special comfort from these words spoken by Jesus.

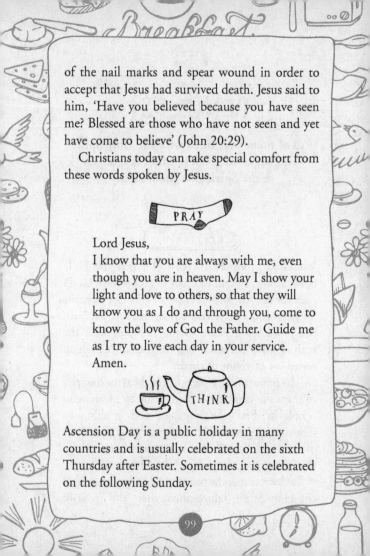

PRAY

Lord Jesus,
I know that you are always with me, even though you are in heaven. May I show your light and love to others, so that they will know you as I do and through you, come to know the love of God the Father. Guide me as I try to live each day in your service.
Amen.

THINK

Ascension Day is a public holiday in many countries and is usually celebrated on the sixth Thursday after Easter. Sometimes it is celebrated on the following Sunday.

PENTECOST

**All of them were filled with the Holy Spirit
and began to speak in other languages,
as the Spirit gave them ability.**

Acts 2:4

REFLECTION

Jesus had promised the disciples that the Holy
Spirit would be sent to them to accomplish God's
plan for the world. At Pentecost (the Greek name
for Shavuot, the Jewish spring harvest festival),
the Holy Spirit came to the disciples with the
rush of a violent wind and tongues of fire which
rested on each one of them.

The power of the Holy Spirit enabled the disciples
to share the good news about Jesus by speaking to
people in their own languages and in this way,
Christianity spread, ultimately reaching all corners
of the world. For this reason, Pentecost is sometimes
thought of as the birthday of the Christian Church.

Paul wrote that the hearts of Christians contained
the Holy Spirit, telling them that: 'the Spirit of

God dwells in you' (Romans 8:9) and the power of the Holy Spirit can be felt when we come to God in prayer.

We can't all go out to tell people of the world about Jesus in their own languages, but we can be open about our Christianity and show the love of Jesus to those we meet.

Almighty God,
I pray that I may be filled with the Holy Spirit and through his power, show the spark of your love within me, reaching out to others in your name. Help me to grow in your service and transform my life in the name of the risen Christ.
Amen.

Pentecost is celebrated seven weeks after Easter Sunday.

Do you know about the work of The Bible Society, which provides Bibles in many languages and sends them to people around the world?

ALL SAINTS

**To all God's beloved in Rome, who are called
to be saints: Grace to you and peace from
God our Father and the Lord Jesus Christ.**

Romans 1:7

Paul is writing to the church in Rome, before a
planned visit.

He believes that God's plan is to bring the
whole of the human race to Christianity. Paul says
that all those within the church are God's chosen
ones because they have accepted God's message
through his Son.

In his first letter to the Corinthians, Paul refers
to the church as 'those who are sanctified in Christ
Jesus, called to be saints' (1 Corinthians 1:2).

There were many martyrs in the early Church
and there have been many across the years. All
Saints' Day honours those who have given
their lives in martyrdom, or in service to others

because of their faith. We have an opportunity to remember them.

PRAY

Almighty God,
I give you thanks for all the saints who
have suffered and given their lives to
your service. Their courage, sacrifice and
dedication inspire me, showing me that
faith with love can overcome all challenges.
Today, I particularly remember
the life of . . . . . .
Amen.

THINK

Is there a particular saint that you feel close to or inspired by?

Do you share a name or birthday with a saint?

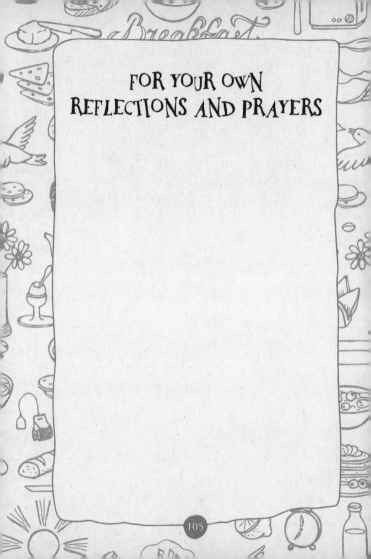

FOR YOUR OWN
REFLECTIONS AND PRAYERS